PREFACE

This set of three anthems by Maurice Greene (1696–1755), published by the Church Music Society to mark the 75th anniversary of its inauguration in 1906, has been newly edited from the original collection of *Forty Select Anthems*, which appeared in London in 1743. The subsequent, revised editions of ?1745 and 1770 have also been consulted.

Abbreviations in the source text have been amplified, misprints rectified, and punctuation rendered consistent, without further reference. The commentary below draws attention to instances of unclear or ambiguous underlay. Editorial slurs are shown thus:

Original note-values have been retained and also – except where noted below – original barring. The interpretation of appoggiaturas notated as grace-notes is specified, in all cases, in the commentary. Note-groupings have been made regular, superfluous accidentals omitted, and *fermata* added where these are not included in the source.

All editorial matter is printed in small type or within square brackets. The ranges of the respective voice-parts are indicated at the beginning of each movement, as are suggested metronome markings – intended only as an approximate guide. 'Solo' has been substituted for Greene's designation 'verse', and 'full' for 'chorus', in the vocal parts.

The notation of the continuo figuring follows present-day practice. Figures in italics are supplied from the editions of ?1745 and 1770.

The realization of the continuo bass for organ (manuals only) is editorial. In the interests of preserving line and texture in the keyboard writing, a harmony note referred to by the figures may occasionally be missing from the organ continuo if it is already present in a voice-part or if the harmonic sense is sufficiently explicit without it. Also, one or two vocal appoggiaturas are doubled or otherwise accommodated in the continuo part, although figures are lacking.

I should like to thank Watkins Shaw and David Rowland for kindly helping in the preparation of this edition.

April 1981

Richard Marlow
Cambridge

COMMENTARY

1   O GOD OF MY RIGHTEOUSNESS

ANTHEM for 2 Voices. PSALM IV.

Text   Largo Andante: verse 1
Adagio-Andante-Adagio: verses 2 & 3 (parts only)
Largo Andante: verse 9
Andante: verses 5 & 4 (part only)

2.org: since the G appears as a semiquaver, double dotting may be intended during this movement. The opening bars of each part, in this alternative reading, are indicated by editorial rhythm-signs above the staves / 11.org.beat 2: figures $\frac{6}{5}$ / 14.org.beat 1: figures $\frac{5}{3}$ / 60.ten & 62.sop & ten: elision of syllables editorial / 98, 112 & 114.sop.beat 2: D (or G) appoggiaturas added to coincide with continuo harmony, following Greene's cadential practice elsewhere / 120.org.beat 1: figuring $\frac{7}{\flat}$ ($\flat$ misplaced) / 130.org: figuring aligned with quaver F, 7$\natural$ ($\natural$ misplaced) / 134.org: figuring aligned with 2nd quaver F, $\frac{6}{4}$ / 141–2.org: figuring included but inaccurately aligned in 1743.

Appoggiaturas printed as grace-notes in the source have been interpreted as follows:

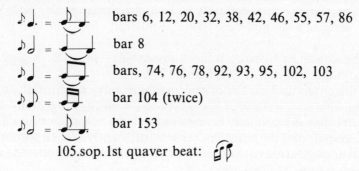

bars 6, 12, 20, 32, 38, 42, 46, 55, 57, 86

bar 8

bars, 74, 76, 78, 92, 93, 95, 102, 103

bar 104 (twice)

bar 153

105.sop. 1st quaver beat:

2   BLESSED ARE THOSE THAT ARE UNDEFILED IN THE WAY

ANTHEM for two Voices. PSALM CXIX. 1st Part.

Text   Largo: verses 1 & 2
Recitative: verse 4
Andante: verses 5 & 18
Vivace: verses 15 & 16
Vivace: verses 171 & 172

In the Andante movement the composer may well have intended the rhythm to be interpreted in a more relaxed manner as , particularly in juxtaposition with the triplet-quaver sequences.

114.sop2: no B appoggiatura / 168.ten & 171.bass: underlay slurs confused / 174.sop2: no D appoggiatura / 183.ten & bass: underlay unclear / 185.org: 'verse' brought forward from the beginning of bar 186.

Appoggiaturas printed as grace-notes in the source have been interpreted as follows:

bars 3, 6, 38, 114, 116, 134, 136, 138

bars 17, 22, 24, 56, 72, 82, 88, 130, 132, 152, 164, 174, 184, 191, 197, 201, 210, 216, 232, 234

bars 24, 39, 55, 62

bar 227.alto

3   LET MY COMPLAINT COME BEFORE THEE, O LORD

FULL ANTHEM for 5 Voices. Psalm CXIX, last Part.

Text   Largo: verses 169 & 170
        Andante: verses 171 & 172

All time-signatures are editorial / 8.org: figure 7 aligned with minim G / 17–18: one bar only in source / 25.org.3rd minim beat: figures $^6_4$ / 42.alto: slur misplaced over previous C–B♮ pair / 43–44.ten & 47–48.sop2: slur over B♭–C crotchets only /54.sop2: E♭ for D / 59.2nd minim beat – 60.1st minim beat.org: right-hand part a 3rd too low / 65–67: editorial barring. At 65 Greene has a bar of two minims' duration, followed by two bars of four minims' worth. He inserts another bar lasting two minims half-way through 67 to restore the $^4_2$ sequence thereafter / 69 & 71.bass: minims G–C slurred.

Appoggiaturas printed as grace-notes in the source have been interpreted as follows:

bar 25

bars 30, 70, 72

CHURCH MUSIC SOCIETY REPRINTS No. 57
Honorary General Editor: Richard Marlow

THREE ANTHEMS
by
MAURICE GREENE
(1696–1755)

1   O GOD OF MY RIGHTEOUSNESS
     Verse anthem for soprano and tenor soloists,
     S.A.T.B. chorus, and organ continuo

2   BLESSED ARE THOSE THAT ARE UNDEFILED IN THE WAY
     Verse anthem for two soprano soloists,
     S.A.T.B. chorus, and organ continuo

3   LET MY COMPLAINT COME BEFORE THEE, O LORD
     Full anthem for S.S.A.T.B. chorus and organ continuo

Edited by
Richard Marlow

Published for the
CHURCH MUSIC SOCIETY
by
OXFORD UNIVERSITY PRESS
WALTON STREET OXFORD OX2 6DP

CONTENTS

1. O GOD OF MY RIGHTEOUSNESS

Verse anthem for soprano and tenor soloists, S.A.T.B. chorus, and organ continuo

MAURICE GREENE
Forty Select Anthems, London, 1743,
Volume Two, *pp* 79–84
Edited by Richard Marlow

Verses from Psalm IV

*See commentary, p. iv

Printed in Great Britain

2

Three Anthems

3

4

6

8

Three Anthems

10

12

* This phrase may have to be transferred to the tenor part.

Three Anthems

2. BLESSED ARE THOSE THAT ARE UNDEFILED IN THE WAY

Verse anthem for two soprano soloists, S.A.T.B. chorus, and organ continuo

MAURICE GREENE
Forty Select Anthems, London, 1743
Volume Two, pp 1–8
Edited by Richard Marlow

Verses from Psalm CXIX

Printed in Great Britain

Oxford University Press
Walton St., Oxford OX2 6DP

18

keep, __ that I might keep thy sta - tutes; O that my ways were made so di - rect, __ that I might keep, that I might keep thy sta - tutes. O - pen thou mine eyes, o - pen thou mine eyes, that I may see the won - - drous things, __ the won-drous things of thy _____ law; O that my ways were made so di - rect, __ that I might keep, that I might keep __ thy

* See commentary, p. iv

Three Anthems

Three Anthems

talk,   will I talk of thy com‑mand‑ments, and have_ res‑pect   un‑to   thy

‑mand‑ments, and have   res‑pect,   and have_ res‑pect_ un‑to   thy

ways,   and have res‑pect un‑to   thy ways.   My   de‑light shall be in thy_

ways,   and have res‑pect un‑to   thy   ways.

___ sta‑tutes,   my   de‑light shall be, my de‑light shall be, shall

My   de‑light shall   be in thy   sta‑tutes, my de‑light shall be, my de‑light shall

* Solo range

Three Anthems

3. LET MY COMPLAINT COME BEFORE THEE, O LORD

Full anthem for S.S.A.T.B. chorus and organ continuo

MAURICE GREENE
Forty Select Anthems, London, 1743,
Volume Two, *pp* 25–29
Edited by Richard Marlow

Verses from Psalm CXIX

Printed in Great Britain

38

Processed and printed by
Halstan & Co. Ltd., Amersham, Bucks., England